# Racism

## Divided by Color

# Racism

## Divided by Color

**Gerald Newman and
Eleanor Newman Layfield**

*—Multicultural Issues—*

**ENSLOW PUBLISHERS, INC.**

44 Fadem Road          P.O. Box 38
Box 699                      Aldershot
Springfield, N.J. 07081  Hants GU12 6BP
U.S.A.                          U.K.

*In memory of our parents, Lillie and Harry Newman,*
*and Martin Weintraub.*
*For Edith Weintraub,*
*W. David, Bevin and Aaron.*

Copyright © 1995 by Gerald Newman and Eleanor Newman Layfield.

**Library of Congress Cataloging-In-Publication Data**

Newman, Gerald.
      Racism: Divided by Color / Gerald Newman, Eleanor Newman Layfield.
         p. cm. —(Multicultural Issues)
      Includes bibliographical references (p. ) and index.
      Summary: A look at the history of and societal factors
involved in racism, as well as how to deal with prejudice
against people based on skin color and its manisfestations.
      ISBN 0-89490-641-0
      1. Racism—Juvenile literature. 2. Racism—United States—
Juvenile literature. [1. Racism.] I. Layfield, Eleanor Newman.
II Title. III. Series.
HT1521.N47 1995
305.8—dc20                     94-38963
                                    CIP
                                      AC

Printed in the United States of America.

10 9 8 7 6 5 4 3 2 1

**Photo Credits:** Anti-Defamation League, pp. 40, 42, 61, 63; Library of Congress,
pp. 13, 20, 27, 29, 47, 53, 72, 77, 80, 86, 98, 100.

**Cover Photo:** Photo Edit/David Young-Wolff.

# Contents

# Acknowledgments:

*The authors would like to thank the following people for their help:*

Bevin Bauman, Aaron Newman

Thomas Halpern and Jane Orhauer, ADL

Maya Keech and Debra Evans, Library of Congress

Theresa Lo Monaco, Karen Funtleyder, Harry Weinstein, and the entire Upward Bound Class at High School of Redirection, Brooklyn, New York

# Introduction

The idea of disliking people because of the color of their skin has existed as far back as history has been recorded. Perhaps the word *racism* hadn't been coined yet, but certainly concerned reactions to strangers or outsiders have always existed.

## *Imagine this:*

A stranger approaches a group. The group members move toward each other and immediately surround their young. There is apparent curiosity about the stranger. The stranger may look, smell, or move differently. The group members wonder: Why is this stranger here? Is this stranger harmful? Does the stranger want our possessions, our young, our mates? Is the stranger a threat? Their conclusion is that the stranger probably is a threat. Then they think: We must protect ourselves. We must protect our possessions, our young, our mates. We must rid ourselves of this stranger. Consider the following:

## Scenario I

Here the group is a flock of birds that like to eat nectar from flowers. But there are not many nectar-bearing flowers left. Then another bird swoops down looking for nectar. This bird is not a member of their flock. The group is threatened by the stranger because their food source is scarce. Instantly, their wings spread, their heads lunge forward, and they drive the stranger away.[1]

## Scenario 2

The group is composed of humans. When a stranger approaches, there is likely to be a sense of group concern. The group wants to know who the stranger is and why he or she came. Though there may be similarities between the stranger and group members, the stranger doesn't look or sound or dress like the others. Sensing differences and afraid of what the differences might mean, the group does not want the stranger among them.

Did you notice what these groups had in common? The common thread is an apprehension or fear of the stranger. This fear and hatred of strangers or foreigners (or anything strange or foreign) is called xenophobia (*xeno* from the Greek word "xenos," meaning stranger, and *phobia* from the Latin for fear).[2] Xenophobia is common to all birds and mammals as part of a protection system to ensure survival of the group.[3]

## *Bigotry*

Humans innately exhibit all the characteristics of xenophobia, but they sometimes take xenophobia a step further. They heighten the fear of the group against the stranger by using negative descriptive words. Words such as "different," "weird," "sneaky," "stingy," "crazy," "lazy," "stupid," "dirty," and "arrogant" are powerful, even though they may not be applicable or true. In fact, even in the face of the truth, the group's opinion of the stranger will not change. The group may use words that are much worse and far more hurtful to the stranger. All the while the group keeps finding more reasons to keep the stranger out.

Xenophobia has now evolved into *bigotry*. Bigotry is an obstinate or blind attachment to a particular belief, unreasonable enthusiasm in favor of a party, sect, or opinion; excessive prejudice, intolerance.[4]

## Racism

The power of words can continue to build. Each negative remark made by the group about the stranger indicates to the members of the group that *they* do not exhibit those negative traits. For instance, if the stranger is called stupid, the members of the group think they are smart. If the stranger is called ugly, then it stands to reason that the members of the group are beautiful. If the stranger is called lazy, the group members are industrious. The power of words has transformed the members of the group into people who think they are superior to the stranger. Now, suppose the group turns all its feelings of hatred and superiority against the stranger because of the color of the stranger's skin. Xenophobia and bigotry have now led to racism: "any attitude, belief, behavior, or institutional arrangement that tends to favor one race or ethnic group over another."[5]

One of the earliest recorded theories of racism can be traced to the Bible, in the story of Ham, the son of Noah. As described in Genesis 9 and 10, Ham was black. He angered Noah, who thought Ham was disobedient. In a rage, Noah cursed Ham's son Canaan: "A slave of slaves shall he be to his brothers." This story has been interpreted by some to suggest that blacks were disobedient and destined to a life of slavery.

Just such an inference was made in 1500 by George Best, an English adventurer, " . . . some naturall [*sic*] infection of the first inhabitants of that country [Africa] and so all the whole progenie [*sic*] of them descended, are still polluted with the same blot of infection."[6]

Abraham Lincoln said the following words when asked what the status of black people would be in the aftermath of freeing the slaves: "I am not nor ever have been in favor of bringing about in any way the social and political equality of the white and black races."[7]

In 1882, United States Senator John Franklin Miller made this remark on the floor of the Senate: "Let us keep pure the blood which circulates through our political system . . . and preserve our national life from the gangrene of the oriental civilization."[8]

Although the statement of Lincoln, who said blacks and whites were not equal; and the remark of Senator Miller, who compared Asians to a condition such as gangrene (which rots human tissue), would not be acceptable today, there is still disagreement on the extent of racism in the United States. This is because people have differing opinions on what racism is. What some people may think is unobjectionable behavior may seem to be racist to others.

There are four types of racism which fall under the following broad definition: any attitude, belief, behavior, or institutional arrangement that tends to favor one race or ethnic group over another.

## Attitudinal Racism

This is a general dislike of a certain racial or ethnic group. This kind of racism occurs when people can find no reason for disliking certain groups, they just do.

## Ideological Racism

These are theories or set beliefs directly stating that some races are superior to others. An example is Adolf Hitler's theory of Aryan Superiority.

## Individual and/or Group Discrimination

These are behaviors of individuals and/or groups that lead to unequal treatment based on race. Examples are when a person is not allowed to enter a store or hotel only because of the color of his or her skin or when taxicab drivers will not pick up certain fares because of the color of their skin. Also included in this category is racially motivated violence; an example is a 1992 incident in Florida when three white men deliberately set fire to a black man.

## Institutional Racism

Institutional racism goes beyond individual and/or group thoughts and actions. In this case, social institutions such as family, church, school, business, and government create patterns of injustice and inequality based on the color of a person's skin. Often individuals involved with these institutions may be unaware that they are participating in racism. An example of this kind of racism is the high cost of college tuition. The high cost keeps more blacks out of colleges than it does whites. Another example is the higher number of blacks in prison as compared to whites.[9]

In addition to institutional, attitudinal, ideological, and individual and/or group racism, we have overt racism. People involved in this form of racism are fully aware of what they are doing.

The Civil Rights Act of 1964 was implemented to combat all forms of racism. This act specifically prohibits discrimination based on race in housing, education, and employment. Yet, more than thirty years later, it appears that racism has not yet been eliminated.

World events, such as the disintegration of the Communist bloc countries, and intense poverty in other countries have resulted in a new wave of immigrants to the shores of the United States. Fear and mistrust of these people, with their different skin colors and cultural identities, add to the racism that continues to plague our nation.

Institutional racism effectively prohibited African Americans from voting in government elections until 1965. The man shown here is registering to vote in Canton, Mississippi, in 1965.

Recent events halfway around the world point to the fact that racism can destroy not only individuals, but it also has the power to destroy an entire nation. In South Africa, the policy of apartheid—a government policy of strict segregation and political and economic discrimination against native blacks and other people of color—was practiced by the white people who held political power. Until that policy was abandoned in 1993, there was no peace in South Africa; the country was, in fact, almost destroyed as blacks began to fight for their rights after more than two hundred years of apartheid.

One way we can ensure this will not happen here is to educate ourselves about the nature of racism and what we can do to stem its growth and do away with it.

# The Concept of Race

"Sticks and stones may break my bones, but names will never hurt me"—in today's world this old saying is not necessarily true. In an age when communication moves with the speed of light, it is important that what we say does not become misinterpreted. Words can and do hurt!

The concept of race has often been misunderstood and has sometimes been misused on purpose. Biology has been confused with culture, language, nationality, or religion. Differences in physical appearances have led people to believe that some groups have more or less intelligence, talent, or morality than others.

The word race has roots in Latin: *generatio*, or a begetting; in French: *race*, family; and in Italian: *razza*, family. According to *Webster's New Universal Unabridged Dictionary*, race is defined as "(a) any of the major biological divisions of mankind, distinguished by color and texture of hair, color of skin and eyes, stature, bodily proportions, etc.; many ethnologists now consider that there are only three primary divisions, the Caucasian (loosely, *white race*) Negroid (loosely, *black race*), and Mongoloid (loosely, *yellow race*) each with various subdivisions, . . . the term has acquired so many unscientific connotations that in this sense it is often replaced in scientific usage by ethnic stock or group."[1]

There have been different concepts of race classification over the years, some of which have been disproved or changed as new information became available. The following are some popular theories:

## Three-Race Theory

The definition of race in which all people are placed in one of three primary divisions is used as the basis of the "three-race theory." This theory is useful as long as scientists believe that all people belong to only one of three races, and that the traits of each race are "immutable," that is, those traits can't be transferred from one race to another. However, it is important to remember some physical facts. For example, not every Asian is yellow, and some do not have an epicanthic lid (an extra fold of skin over the eyelid). Members of the Caucasian race are represented by many variations of "white" skin. Some blacks do not have the lip form or the hair form that conformed to the original criteria set by scientists for the Negroid race.

## The Theory of Evolution

The three-race system of classification started to lose favor as biologists began to accept the theory of evolution. World explorers were proving the three-race system weak as they discovered humans who did not exactly fit criteria for one of the three races. Biologists were meanwhile questioning long-held theories that species of plants and animals did not change over long periods of time.

Paleontologists (scientists who study past geological periods by studying fossil remains) were also coming up with information supporting the theory of evolution. The fossils at first looked very much like their modern-day counterparts, but when they were studied carefully, they did not really match. Scientists thus concluded that species of plants and animals could change over time. But they didn't know how these changes occurred.

It was Charles Darwin, in his book, *The Origin of Species* (1859), who theorized that populations of organisms could change over time as they adapted to the environment around them. This thought was the basis of Darwin's theory of natural selection which accounts for why some members of species survive and others do not.[2]

Adapting this theory to the three-race system of classification led scientists to the conclusion that what were once considered natural traits of the three races, were really adaptations that occurred over time as a result of environmental conditions.

## The Population Approach

The method of classification called the population approach appeared in the early 1900s, when scientists saw that widely separated groups could develop similar characteristics by adapting to environments that were similar, even if their ancestors were different. For instance, the Quecha Indians of the Andes and the Sherpas of the Himalayas are not related. But both groups have similar physical characteristics because they adapted to life in the same kind of high mountain environment. Mountain dwellers have larger lungs than people who live at lower altitudes because there is less oxygen to breathe at higher altitudes.

Anthropologists define a population as "a group of similar people who are more likely to mate with one another than with outsiders."[3] When scientists analyze populations, they investigate clusters of physical traits, such as the larger lungs of the mountain dweller or the lack of type O blood in some central Asian populations.

Scientists using the population approach make no assumptions based on race. They see each population as the result of a unique set of circumstances, which include:

- Adaptation, or a change in structure, function, or form that produces a better adjustment of an animal or plant to its environment.

- Genetic change, or a change in the elements that determine hereditary characteristics, which may be due to adaptation.

- Isolation, or the ability of a population to keep apart from other populations because of the environment.

- History of Migration, or the ability of a population to move from one area to another and adapt to the new area's environment.

## Classifying by Race

While some scientists have abandoned the idea of classifying human beings into races, the average person continues to identify himself or herself, as well as others, as members of a particular race. One reason for this is because governmental institutions continue to use racial classifications in the majority of its statistical reports and analyses. In fact, everyone expects the government to present conclusions of census reports in terms of race. For instance, the government can tell you which racial groups earn the most income. It also can tell you which racial groups have seen an increase in income. Or it can tell you what racial groups have moved from the city to the suburbs or the reverse.

These statistics need interpretation, however, and that's when the trouble can start. Compare the following two headlines:

"White-Black Disparity in Income Narrowed in 80's, Census Shows" (*The New York Times*, July 24, 1992).

"Income Equality Gap Widens for Minorities" (*USA Today*, July 24, 1992).[4]

John F. Kennedy was very much involved in the struggle to provide African Americans with equal job opportunities. He is shown here with those involved in the March on Washington for Jobs and Freedom. This took place in August 1963.

These headlines were based on the same government data. How can the same data result in such different conclusions? One headline gives us reason to believe that racism may be declining since incomes of blacks and whites are not so far apart. But the other headline confuses the issue. Does *USA Today* want its readers to believe that all minorities, including blacks, are not making as much money as whites? If readers didn't see the headline in *The New York Times*, they might believe that racism might be the cause of the lack of equality in income.

What if the government decided one day to eliminate racial classification? There must be other ways to evaluate people, such as income, family size, home ownership, occupation, and education. Yet, any system of classification brings with it, preconceived ideas about each of the categories. There are no easy answers to the problems of racism.

# Tracing Racism Throughout History

*[History] shows us that all civilizations derive from the white race . . .*
—Joseph Arthur, comte de Gobineau, 1915.[1]

Joseph Arthur, comte (or count) de Gobineau, was a French writer and diplomat who promoted certain ideas of social and racial behavior. In particular, de Gobineau believed in the superiority of the "white" race, although he had no factual support for his belief. Furthermore, his definition of the white race did not include white people who lived in southern and eastern Europe. The white race, to de Gobineau, was represented only by people who were tall, blond, blue-eyed Nordic Europeans, who must provide all the leaders and leadership of the world. For these reasons, Joseph Arthur, comte de Gobineau, was known as the "father of modern racism."[2]

While we may not agree with de Gobineau's point of view, we can try to understand why he might have made the statement he did. History provides some clues. Certain events occurring throughout the world during his time did have an influence on how people of one race viewed people of another race. These events could be listed as follows:

- The onset of trade and exploration

- Wars

- Slavery

- The policy of imperialism

- Immigration

## Trade and Exploration

With the beginning of trade to various unexplored parts of the world, it was inevitable that people would encounter other people who looked different. Just as inevitable was the resulting xenophobia on both sides; the Chinese, for instance, described the Dutch as "a race of blond haired, green-eyed barbarians that [they] thought were directly descended from monkeys."[3] One Portuguese explorer, observing Peruvian Indians in South America, wrote in his diary that "their chief desire is to eat, drink, worship heathen idols, and commit bestial obscenities . . . "[4]

But the feelings of xenophobia and distaste on the part of both the Chinese and the Dutch were quickly overcome as the traders realized the enormous profits to be made in trading with each other. On the other hand, the Portuguese explorer didn't hesitate for a moment to use the labor of "heathen savages" to carry away all his goods for his return trip to Portugal. In North America, traders and explorers viewed the natives of this new land in a similar manner. Because they were "red-skinned savages," "worshippers of trees and birds" and barely clothed, the natives were deemed to be inferior by the explorers. Perhaps that was all the justification the explorers and settlers needed to take the natives' land.

## War and Slavery

As trade grew between groups of people who lived near each other and those living oceans away, skirmishes were inevitable; and those skirmishes sometimes became wars. The spoils of war could be material valuables or human beings who would often become slaves to the victors. When the Romans expanded their empire into northern Europe, they quickly conquered the inhabitants, whom they called "barbarians," or barely human. Those barbarians who survived the journey from their own lands to Rome were then sold as slaves.

In ancient times, slaves were often of the same race as their masters. In fact, in some instances, slaves were better educated than their masters. Aesop, the poet who wrote *Aesop's Fables*, as well as Terence, a writer of history, had once been a slave. War could subject very civilized men to servitude. The only difference between the slave and his master was the freedom denied to the slave. In such cases, when a slave was finally freed, no one could tell the difference between the slave and his master.

This was not to be the case in the United States. The settlers there needed a tremendous workforce to farm and cultivate their land, but they could not use Native Americans to perform the labor. Because the Native Americans knew the land better than the settlers, the former could easily escape, and it was too expensive to recapture them. Instead, at first settlers used other settlers as indentured servants. This type of servant would work to pay off his or her passage to America, which took from seven to ten years. At the end of that time, they were free. They could then become paid servants to their masters, or they could buy their own land and farm it for themselves. Settlers who fell into debt sometimes ended up in servitude until they were debt-free, but, for the most part, there were just enough people to work the land. However, an alternative presented itself.

By the eighth century, African slaves were being exported by Arabs, who had conquered Northern Africa. Africans were also sold to Spanish and Portuguese traders.[5]

By the early seventeenth century, the Portuguese had already explored the coast of West Africa and were themselves involved in delivering slaves to the British West Indian colonies. Thus African slaves seemed to be the solution to the manpower shortage in the United States, so they were brought here against their will.

According to historians, the first African captives were brought over on a Dutch ship in 1619, to Jamestown, Virginia. These first captives were treated as indentured servants or contract laborers just as the Europeans settlers were. But,

The African slave trade took Africans captive and transported them against their will from their African homelands to the United States to serve as indentured servants.

by the mid-seventeenth century, some Southern colonies passed laws that decreed all incoming Africans would be slaves forever.

The difference between slavery in ancient times and slavery during the colonization of America is that in the United States, slavery would forever be linked to race. Since all slaves were considered inferior to their masters, Africans in America would thus be considered inferior.

Given the rules under which African slaves had to live, it was inevitable that they would confirm the stereotypes the slave owners held, becoming a self-fulfilling prophecy. If anyone were forcibly removed from their families and their country, transported to another country, where they did not understand the language and were dependent on their masters for their very existence, one would expect those people to be docile and childlike. They would have little knowledge because they were forbidden to learn to read, and also knew they could suffer the loss of a finger if they wanted to learn to write. That was the story of the Africans who were brought to America. They had no last names of their own. They were a commodity, and they weren't white.

Slavery in the United States began as a solution to a severe labor shortage. It quickly became complicated by the reaction of white people to people of color. It was so easy to consider those enslaved as less than human, unlike any other group who was enslaved throughout history. The fact that Africans would always be associated with slavery because of the color of

Slavery in the United States began as a solution to a severe labor shortage. It brought with it, however, problems that would effect this country for hundreds of years.

their skin left America and Americans to struggle with unforeseen difficulties for hundreds of years.

Alexis de Tocqueville, a French historian noted for his observations of America in *Democracy in America*, written more than one hundred years ago, recognized this "unique difficulty." He wrote that the mere presence of blacks on United States soil would be an embarrassment "now and in the future." His comment was insightful. It was as if he could foretell the problems between whites and blacks in the aftermath of the Civil War, although he died in 1859, two years before the war began. He said the unique difficulty in America was that "servitude is linked to race." He continued, "memories of servitude disgrace the race, and race will forever perpetuate memories of slavery."[6]

While the Civil War began over economic conflicts and ended in efforts to abolish slavery, the Thirteenth Amendment to the Constitution did abolish slavery. The Civil Rights Act of 1866 declared blacks had the same rights of citizenship as whites. Yet as we enter into the twenty-first century, it seems we still hear an echo of de Tocqueville's words—racism and racist practices persist in the face of all the legislation enacted to overcome it. As de Tocqueville said, it is far easier to change the law then it is to change people's minds.

## Imperialism

The colonization of America was also driven, or justified, by the concept of imperialism. Imperialism is the policy of a country by which it seeks to establish control over other countries in order to "civilize" them. While some may question the so-called humanitarian motive behind this great need to civilize the world, racism helped to spread imperialistic actions just as imperialism created racism.

Between the fifteenth century and the middle of the eighteenth century, England, France, the Netherlands, Portugal, Spain, and Germany built imperialistic empires, with colonies in America, India, and Africa. During this period, racial stereotyping became the reason for the colonizing countries to conquer and expand.

Spanish explorers had no problem taking land away from the native South Americans. The "red" color of their skin automatically meant they were inferior. Beneath the conqueror's disdain for people of color was their belief in their own superiority.

In the late nineteenth and early twentieth century, this sense of racial superiority was expressed in the writings of the famous author and poet, Rudyard Kipling.

Kipling may have wanted to help "backward" people to be free from disease and hunger. However, he implied that no matter what the white man does for the "natives," the natives will return to their lazy, irreligious ways, because they were not intelligent enough to realize what was being done for them (or to them). This belief that trying to civilize natives was a hopeless effort was the white man's "burden." It was also a clear example of attitudinal racism (defined in the Introduction).

## Immigration

While America is called a nation of immigrants, some of those who immigrated to its shores, or were brought here against their will, were and still are subject to racism, whether it is openly expressed—overt racism—or it becomes the basis for social and government policy—institutional racism.

During colonial times and until the end of the eighteenth century, immigrants who freely came to America were primarily from northern and western Europe. The English, Scots, German, Irish, Welsh, and Scandinavians came to America in large numbers. They were all white, but their language, culture, and religious beliefs were different. However, they all came to America in the hope of a better life.

## Immigrants and Overt Racism

At the beginning of the 1900s, the nature of those immigrating to the United States began to change. New waves of immigrants arrived from southern and eastern Europe: Italians, Poles, Hungarians, Rumanians, and Russians. They also came to America with the promise that life would be better here, but some social and political scientists did not consider these people "white." Their skin was darker than northern Europeans; their noses were broader. They were Roman Catholic, Eastern Catholic, and Jewish. Sociologists believed that these new religious groups would not adapt to and understand the "American way" because of their religious beliefs. Once in America they did keep to their own neighborhoods, or "ghettos." You could find Polish people in Chicago, Jews in the Lower East Side of New York, and the Irish in Boston. In these large cities, immigrants could find neighborhoods where people spoke their language and worshipped in the same churches and synagogues. It would take more than one generation for these groups to feel secure enough to move out of the ghettos and assimilate into a more "American" lifestyle.

In addition to those immigrants who came to the east coast of the United States, people from Asia, South America, and Mexico began to arrive on the west coast of the United States.

Politicians and sociologists labeled the immigrants on both coasts "undesirable," "clannish," "secretive," "murderous," "sly," and "evil." The immigrants refused to speak English. It was feared that they would eventually intermarry with the original pure white northern Europeans, the ones Joseph Arthur, comte de Gobineau, spoke about as the superior race. The fear was that the immigrants would "mongrelize" the race. These opinions are examples of overt racism, either by attitude or ideology. The stereotypical labeling, the fear that these immigrants of color would destroy the white race, all were openly expressed.

## Institutional Racism and Immigrants

In response to these beliefs, some American politicians proposed that laws be enacted to set limits on the numbers of new immigrants coming to the United States. This is an example of racism that is institutionalized. Here, the feelings and beliefs of hatred and fear based on the race of certain people, were "legalized" into government policy. But this wasn't the first time that laws were passed that discriminated against certain people.

In 1848, the California legislature enacted a law stating that Peruvian Indians, who were excellent miners, could not work in the California gold mines unless they paid a Foreign Miners' Tax.[7] This was a legal method of making it more difficult for Peruvian Indians to make a living in America. In 1902, the U.S. Congress passed legislation that suspended Chinese immigration. In California again, the state legislature barred Japanese people from owning any land. In 1917, Congress passed a law that all new immigrants had to pass a literacy test. Imagine how many Russians, Greeks, Italians, Japanese, and Chinese could be turned away because they could not speak or write the English language. All of these efforts were directed not only at keeping immigrants out, but ensuring that immigrants would not take jobs away from Americans. It was feared that immigrants would work for far less money than Americans, and Americans would therefore be in danger of losing their jobs.

Following World War I, when much of Europe was in shambles, more immigrants came to America. But in 1924, the National Origins Quota Act was passed, limiting immigration from a foreign country to 2 percent of the specific nationalities already residing in the United States as of 1890. In addition, the bill excluded all Japanese people. Congress was making every effort to ensure the continued purity of the majority white northern European race. Over the years, all of those laws were overturned, yet the white race is still the majority race in the United States.

In California today, a growing political tide is focusing on illegal immigrants from Mexico and other Central American countries. Illegal immigrants often take jobs away from Californians because immigrants will work for lower wages. In addition, these immigrants often come to California to take advantage of health care that is far superior to the care they would receive across the border. But they don't pay taxes to support it. Many illegal immigrants will even give birth to their children in America, because they know that anyone born in America is automatically a citizen and is entitled to its benefits.

In Florida, boatloads of Haitians have been sent back to Haiti or to the United States naval base in Guantanamo Bay, Cuba, because the American government has not lifted an embargo against that country. Just recently, matters in Florida have been further complicated by Cubans immigrating to that state's shores in greater numbers than in the past few years. They are also being sent back to the Guantanamo Bay base, where they will have to share space with Haitians until some policy is finally set to allow them to come here.

Bill O. Hing, an immigration expert at Stanford University Law School, claims that "Some people genuinely worry about the problem of too many immigrants in a stagnant economy, but for most, economics is a diversion. Underneath is race."[8] He states that hate groups such as the Ku Klux Klan like nothing better than to find people who would never think of themselves as racists, agreeing with the enforcement of anti-immigration policies. These are the people the Klan and other hate groups would like to indoctrinate with their literature, which focuses on white superiority and the separation of the races.

# Overt Racism: Individual and Organized Hatred

From today's perspective, it isn't unique that blacks in the South vote, or are waited on by white people. It's no great surprise to see black lawyers, doctors, and astronauts at work in offices, hospitals, and space shuttles. It's hard to imagine the terror felt by blacks in the 1950s and 60s as described by a longtime Mississippi resident, "If I saw a white person coming anywhere near me, I'd avert my eyes and begin to shudder, and I'd get this overwhelming desire to disappear."[1]

The struggle against racism resulted in the Civil Rights Act of 1964, which provided the much needed legislation to tear down the barriers to racial equality in the United States, and held the promise that by the end of the twentieth century, racism would be a thing of the past. But, this has not happened. In spite of the substantial gains for blacks in the

United States, people still find ways to get around the law, both on a one-to-one basis and in organized hate groups.

According to Mario Cuomo, the former governor of New York State, the number of hate groups is on the rise in the United States.[2] The incidence of hate crimes has increased as well. Occurrences of white on black violence, as exemplified by incidents in the Howard Beach and Bensonhurst neighborhoods in New York City in 1986, where young black men were beaten because they were in all-white neighborhoods, and the case of a black man in Florida who was set on fire by two white teenagers in 1992, are examples. Occurrences of black on white crime, such as the sexual assault and beating of a white woman in Central Park by a group of black teenagers in 1989, and the case of a fourteen-year-old white boy who was beaten by four young black men in Wisconsin in 1993, are comparable. These incidents, plus hundreds that were probably not reported or just didn't make the headlines, show that overt racism still persists.

It would seem that every positive step taken to eliminate racism results in a backlash incident of some kind that provides all the proof needed for 92 percent of black people and 87 percent of white people to believe, according to a *Time* magazine poll, that racism is still common in America.

## The Ku Klux Klan

Whenever we hear of opinion polls stating that Americans still believe that racism is far from being overturned in the United States, a large part of the problem can be traced directly to an organized group of white supremacists called the Ku Klux Klan (KKK), originally founded in 1866 and officially disbanded in 1869. After the Civil War when the Southern Confederacy was destroyed, the Ku Klux Klan was committed to keeping blacks under control, by violence, if necessary.

The second Ku Klux Klan (founded in 1915) has as its prime mission to demonstrate outward racism and to keep America free from blacks, Jews, Asians, immigrants, homosexuals, Catholics, or any other group that would destroy the purity of the white race. Its members have gone so far as to brutalize or even murder their victims, usually by burning them, lynching them, bombing them, or burning down their homes and places of business. Though they may have committed these atrocities while wearing their white capes and hoods, or under cover of night, they did so without shame, since they believed that what they did was right.

Ironically, the group began quite innocently. Though there are different versions of the story, most historians agree that in 1865, six poor, bored Confederate veterans in Pulaski, Tennessee, thought it would be fun to create a club. The first suggestions for the club's name were "Merry Six" or "The Pulaski Social Club," but no one was pleased with those names. Someone suggested the Greek word *Kyklos* because it meant "circle" or "band." Since the six young men were of Scotch-Irish ancestry, they added the word "Klan." So Kyklos Klan soon became Ku Klux Klan. To make things more interesting and mysterious, they used sheets (since there was no money to make real costumes) to disguise themselves and

The white sheets that these Klansmen are wearing are reported to have started as a masquerade game. Today they serve to disguise the true identity of the wearers.

their horses. As John Lester, one of the founders, wrote: "Each member provided himself with . . . a white mask . . . with orifices for the eyes and nose; a tall fantastic cardboard hat, so constructed as to increase the wearer's apparent height; a gown or robe of sufficient length to cover the entire person."[3] Once properly dressed and once officers were elected, the six rode off to play their masquerade game.

But they soon discovered the fright they could instill in uneducated, unsophisticated people. Membership seemed like a lot of fun and others were soon inducted through a ceremony complete with blindfolds, dark cellars, and oaths of secrecy, all the trappings of a secret society. Within three months, the Klan grew so large it was forced to move to new headquarters.[4]

Soon Den 2 was created in Alabama. But these Athens, Alabama, members were not as fun-loving as the Pulaski members. They were angry that white teachers had been hired to teach black students. The teachers were accused of treating the children "like human beings." A black student who was accused of being "too friendly with his teacher" was forced out of his home in the middle of the night and dumped into an icy stream.

Suddenly, and from then on, the Klan was no longer a "merry" gang of pranksters. It now became the protector of white supremacy throughout the South.

The membership rosters were soon filled with the names of ex-officers of the disbanded Confederate army. It was a way for them to rekindle the flames of the Confederacy that had

Burning wooden crosses has become a symbol of the fear and terror that the Klansmen instill in their victims.

been snuffed out by the loss of the Civil War, by the passage of the Thirteenth Amendment in 1865 (which officially ended slavery), and by the creation of the Freedman's Bureau, which attempted to aid blacks to reach some sort of self-sufficiency. Also occurring were the forced division of large plantations into plots of farmland that were given to former slaves, the Civil Rights Act of 1866 (which granted "full rights and privileges of citizenship" to all people born in the United States), and finally the Fourteenth Amendment (1868), which forbids any state from depriving "any person of life, liberty or property, without due process; nor deny to any person . . . the equal protection of the law."

In 1870 came the Fifteenth Amendment, which granted the right to vote to all male citizens "regardless of race, color or previous condition of servitude." This sent the KKK on a rampage. Not only were homes, schools, and churches burned, but both blacks and white who supported these rights were mercilessly slaughtered. The violence was so severe that President Ulysses S. Grant had to send in forces to oversee election procedures.[5]

With the burning cross as their symbol, Klansmen combed the south, eager to rid it of undesirables so they could keep America "free for the white man." Black families were regarded with such disrespect that inflicting on them pain or even death didn't matter to these men. There was no remorse. So frightening were these terrorists that black families had specific duties for each member in case of a Klan attack. While men and older boys protected the family, the community elders tried to confuse the attackers by giving them misinformation. The children served as lookouts, and the women guarded the precious weapons and ammunition.[6]

The white supremacists, frightened that allowing blacks to vote would throw the whites out of power, instilled fear into white hearts. They suggested that blacks would take away white land, blacks would become the masters and whites would be the servants, and blacks would marry their white daughters.[7] On election day, ballot boxes were often stolen or burned to ensure that black candidates or white candidates who protected black interests did not win an election. Though many of the Klansmen were known to the public, none were ever brought up on charges, because the courts would be filled with defendants who were noted businessmen, law enforcement officers, dignitaries, legislators, and judges.

Under the presidency of Rutherford B. Hayes, America was becoming an industrial power and interest in minority rights lessened. Federal troops were withdrawn and legislation for equality seemed to have ended. Though in most Southern states blacks were the majority, they were nevertheless still second-class citizens. On the surface, Klan attacks seemed to have subsided, but diehard supremacists now used "states-rights" laws to restrain black advancement. Two of the most infamous were the poll tax law and literacy tests. The poll tax required a fee to be paid months in advance of an "unannounced" election in order to be able to vote. Obviously, it was more difficult for the poor (who were usually black) to come up with the tax, so the poor didn't vote. Those whites who opposed passage of the poll tax laws were suddenly victims of arson and assault and they learned quickly to mind their own business.

Literacy tests, on the surface, seemed like a good idea. After all, how could one vote if one couldn't read the names on the ballot? The truth was, the questions asked, such as "How high is up?" and "How many bubbles are in a bar of soap?," were unanswerable. Those blacks who did find ways of overcoming the illegal tests were suddenly convinced by Klansmen that voting was not really important. Legislation gave black Americans equality, but legislation was written on paper that could be torn up. Blacks were hardly better off than they had been before the Civil War.

As western migration grew, blacks joined the parade of people of all races and nationalities who were building a new and flourishing part of America. While blacks moved west, twenty-three million Europeans were immigrating to the United States. The KKK was there to intimidate them and declare that they were taking jobs away from deserving white Americans. Easiest to attack were the Eastern Europeans, who had darker complexions and so were declared inferior to fairer skinned Western Europeans. So now Jews and Catholics were added to the hate list. On the West Coast, Asians joined the list because white supremacists resented the thousands of Chinese who were hired to lay tracks for the transcontinental railroad. White supremacists in California were actually able to lobby for federal laws that curtailed Chinese immigration and even sent thousands of Chinese back to China. Some Chinese though did settle in Hawaii and others moved east.[8]

The Klan never ceased committing its atrocities on whomever it believed was not a true American. It slipped into the shadows for a number of years, but it was there, nonetheless. It concentrated on attacking unions whose sole purpose was to organize workers (many of whom were black) for better working conditions.

In 1905 a new book, *The Clansman, an Historical Romance of the Ku Klux Klan,* was written by Thomas Dixon, a college-educated minister and member of the North Carolina legislature. Dixon didn't see the KKK as destructive, but remembered them from his youth as hooded white horsemen who were there to protect life as he knew it. To him they were almost knights in shining armor, and that's how he portrayed them in his book. The book became a play and eventually the film, *The Birth of a Nation.*

This film, directed by D. W. Griffith, was the first motion picture with a real plot. A sweeping historical epic told in documentary style, it used film techniques never seen before. The final scene showed a daring, dashing Klansman saving a fragile, white Flora from being raped by a black man. It portrayed white good overcoming black evil and turned even those white people who bore no animosity toward blacks into ardent racists. Even President Woodrow Wilson, who saw the movie at a private screening, thought it was "terribly true." Chief Justice of the Supreme Court Edward White, after he

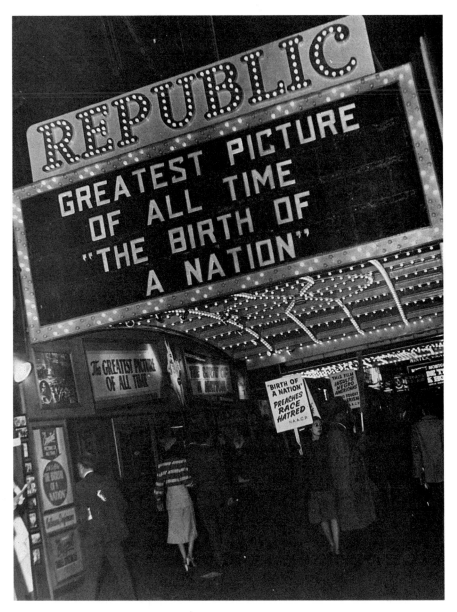

The film entitled "The Birth of a Nation" was taken from a book written by Thomas Dixon. Dixon portrayed the Klan as knights in shining armor. His "vision" of the Klan led to numerous protests.

saw it the following night, told Dixon he had been a member of the KKK.[9]

As the film opened in Atlanta on December 5, 1915, a renewed interest in Klan membership arose. Advertisements to join "a high class order of men of intelligence and character" appeared alongside ads for the film. Led by penniless Methodist minister William Simmons, who placed the ads, the Klan was suddenly reborn as the "Invisible Empire, Knights of the Ku Klux Klan." And *Birth of a Nation* was there to help in its delivery. By 1927, fifty million people had seen it, and, because it seemed to be a documentary, believed every frame of it.

The new Klan spread like brush fire across all forty-eight states, picking up frightened, easily coerced members who marveled at the glittering robes, mammoth parades, and firelight inductions. They gladly paid $10 for initiation and $6 for a hood and gown. Another asset for the Klan was the free publicity the press gave it every time another splashy public function was held.

When called before Congress to defend his violence, Simmons appeared to be a gentle, soft-spoken fatherly type. "He swore the KKK never engaged in violence, always obeyed the Constitution and laws, and stood for 'straight Americanism.' He appeared charming."[10]

The Klan used the Great Depression, which began in 1929, as another excuse to spew out its hatred. Out-of-work true Americans were being displaced by Catholic immigrants, they said, because the pope had infiltrated the American government and was wielding his power to control our country. The Klan claimed that there also existed a Jewish conspiracy to take over the country. Because of the toll the Depression took on so many lives and because of the influx of so many Europeans at the same time, it was easy for the Klan to instill fear in so many poor, usually uneducated and unemployed laborers that Catholics and Jews from foreign lands were taking jobs away from them.[11] Xenophobia coupled with the power of language swept across America again.

Though the Klan claimed to have over two million members and collected nearly $40 million in 1925, by 1929 it was sliding into oblivion (though it didn't completely disappear). People became disillusioned because they noticed that Klan leaders became richer while they remained the same. They saw their leaders preaching godliness while they performed the most ungodly acts. They were threatened with Catholic, Jewish, and Russian takeovers of America but began to realize that none of it ever happened.

In the 1930s three political movements—Communism, Fascism, and Nazism—were on the rise in Europe. The Klan easily associated itself with the Nazis in Germany, who also were eager to see the total annihilation of Jews, Catholics, dissidents, homosexuals, anyone who did not project a lily-white, wholesome image. They were also closely allied to the Italian Fascists who were openly eliminating Jews, Communists, and labor unions in Italy. But there were differences among the three groups. The Fascists and the Nazis were run by professional hate mongers, whereas the KKK was only loosely connected and organized by people who led double lives.

Additionally, the hard times of the 1920s and 1930s and World War II in the 1940s brought Americans together. To many people, racial differences became less important. After World War II and into the mid-1950s, America enjoyed a time of economic prosperity. The Depression was over. New and time-saving consumer goods were being produced. Jobs were available. America was the number-one world power. White and black Americans were ready to make the necessary changes that would put everyone on an equal playing field.

The National Association for the Advancement of Colored People (NAACP) made racism its focus in combating the forces of inequality. It used the courts to make its case for change. In 1954, Thurgood Marshall, later a Supreme Court Justice, and legal scholar Charles Houston, both African American and both members of the NAACP, argued before the United States Supreme Court the case for desegregation of American schools in the landmark *Brown v. Board of Education of Topeka, Kansas* case. Martin Luther King, Jr., and Ralph Abernathy started the Southern Christian Leadership Center and initiated a boycott against Montgomery, Alabama's segregated buses. African Americans began demanding their rights to be served in segregated restaurants. In the face of all this progress, the KKK had all the reasons it needed for renewed hostility. Violence reached new heights. Klansmen ranted that "blood would run in school corridors."[12]

In 1956, hooded Klansmen marched up and down the streets of Montgomery to frighten African Americans who were riding the Montgomery buses. Riders were assaulted and even shot. One Sunday morning bombs destroyed four churches and the homes of the ministers who were involved in the boycott. Martin Luther King, Jr.'s Montgomery Improvement Association was at first blamed. After a trial, the two men who did throw the bombs walked away absolutely free. Next, a carload of Klansmen decided to seek out a black man who was supposedly dating a white woman. However, they found the wrong man and forced him to jump from a bridge to his death. The judge ruled for the defendants because in his view "merely forcing a person to jump does not naturally and probably lead to the death of such a person."[13]

In the first four years after *Brown* v. *Board of Education of Topeka, Kansas* "there were 530 cases of overt racial violence and intimidation—including 6 murders, 29 shootings, 44 beatings, 5 stabbings, and the bombing of 30 homes, 7 churches, 4 synagogues, and 4 schools. . . . Between 1956 and 1963, more than 130 homes, places of worship and businesses had been destroyed or damaged by explosions."[14]

The civil rights movement (which culminated in the Civil Rights Act of 1964) was instrumental in exposing what the KKK was doing to destroy any progress the movement was making. But the killing of Medgar Evers, a field secretary of the Mississippi branch of the NAACP, touched a nerve among both black and white Americans. In September 1962 Evers counseled James Meredith, the first black student to attend the University of Mississippi, the same institution whose law school would not enroll Evers because he was African American. Evers was trying to have the local government adopt fair employment practices. The mayor, however, wouldn't budge and the civil rights workers were getting angry. On May 28, 1963, a group of black and white students seated themselves at a lunch counter. Instead of being served food they were spray painted and doused with salt and pepper. A photograph of the insult, published across the country, forced the mayor to acknowledge Evers' petition. Evers became a hero.

As the movement grew, he had received threats against his life. At one point his house was bombed. Coming home late from a strategy meeting on June 12, 1963, Evers was ambushed in front of his home and shot to death while his children waited for their father to walk in the door. The man who shot him was tried twice for murder and twice the jury did not convict him. The day after Evers' funeral, however, the mayor of Jackson appointed the city's first African-American police officer, one of the things Evers had been fighting for.[15]

Mississippi drew national attention in the summer of 1964. Over 100,000 unemployed African-American men and women and their families, suffering from malnutrition and starvation, lived in cardboard shanties surrounding the rich farmland of two prominent U.S. senators, James O. Eastland and John Stennis. Nothing was done to change the deplorable conditions because, of the 400,000 eligible African-American

Medgar Evers served as a field secretary of the Mississippi branch of the NAACP. As the civil rights movement grew, Evers received threats against his life. He was eventually shot to death in front of his own home. The men who shot him were never convicted.

voters, only 24,000 were registered. There were not enough people who cared enough to vote the politicians out of office. The Council of Federated Organizations, eager to remedy the problem, sent an onslaught of young civil rights workers to Mississippi to register voters. To combat them, the Klan, which had been relatively quiet over the previous few years, reemerged as the White Knights of Mississippi. There were reports of an enormous number of shootings, firebombings, whippings, and deaths. On Sunday night, June 21, 1964, the White Knights burned down the Zion Methodist Church in Meridian, Mississippi. Three young civil rights workers—James Chaney, Andrew Goodman, and Michael Schwerner—were organizing a Freedom School, a place for civil rights activities, in that church.[16]

It was James Chaney who had convinced the reluctant church officials to allow them to use the church. Twenty-one-year-old Chaney was a member of the Congress of Racial Equality (CORE). Andrew Goodman, also twenty-one, and Michael Schwerner, twenty-five, were New Yorkers who had volunteered to come to Mississippi. All three CORE members were experienced in their quest for black equality, but Goodman and Schwerner were hated by the White Knights for being white outsiders and for being Jewish.

One June 22, Chaney was driving Goodman and Schwerner to Philadelphia, Mississippi, when they were stopped by Sheriff Cecil Price. Chaney was charged with speeding, and Goodman and Schwerner were accused of burning down the church as a way of attracting sympathy for their cause. At first they were jailed, but then, without warning, they were told to go back to Meridian. While on the return trip they were stopped again by Price who this time had brought two carloads of White Knights with him. The three young men were taken out and shot and their bodies dumped into a dam construction site. A bulldozer then piled soil over them. The disappearance of the three men set the country in a whirl. The Federal Bureau of Investigation (FBI), the Justice Department, and even President Lyndon Johnson got involved.

Fortunately, an anonymous informer, in exchange for $30,000, described where the three bodies could be found. Bulldozers had to remove ten tons of soil to find the decomposed bodies. On October 20, 1967, seven members of the Klan were found guilty of violating the civil rights of Chaney, Goodman, and Schwerner, while three others were freed by a hung jury. No one was ever charged with murder. The most severe penalty was imprisonment up to ten years. By July 1976, all had been released from jail. But it was the first time a Mississippi jury ever sentenced a Klansmen for committing a murder.[17]

The intervention of the federal government, the zeal of the media, and the disgust of the American public forced the Klan to retreat. But the Klan has not and probably will not ever disappear. Whenever a group believes its rights are being taken away by another group that it considers inferior, bigotry will raise its venomous head and find a leader to urge the ignorant into violence. Integration in public facilities such as schools and transportation, and affirmative action, which allowed blacks advantages over whites in employment and housing to make up for all the years of enslavement, became sore spots for the Klan and reason enough for it to reemerge.

## David Duke

Take the case of David Duke, a member of the Klan since he was seventeen years old. Duke, the son of a State Department engineer, while still a junior at Louisiana State University, "spent part of 1971 teaching English to Laotian army officers." Duke, it was thought, had CIA connections. When an investigation of credentials to be able to run for office was attempted, however, no one seemed to be able to find any answers, even through the Freedom of Information Act. All that was known was that Duke was personable, boyish, good-looking, and bright. Yet while picketing William Kuntsler, the noted civil rights lawyer, he was seen wearing "a storm trooper uniform complete with swastika." In 1975, he was arrested for organizing a group that terrorized police officers in their cars, calling them "commie Jews."

In that same year, after opening the Klan to college students, Duke ran for the state senate in Baton Rouge, Louisiana. Though he lost, his appeal to the young middle class gained him 33 percent of the vote. His campaign centered on opposition to integration, busing, gun control, tax increases, and reverse discrimination. At a Klan rally, Duke "attacked reverse discrimination, black welfare, oppression of the white race, and Jewish control of the media. 'I say if the Jews can have their state in Israel, we can have our state right here in the United States. . . . We have a right as the white majority to run this country as we see fit!'"

Duke's boyishness appeals to young people. He and his aides distributed leaflets at local high schools that cried out: "White Students Fight for White Power! by becoming a member of the Klan Youth Corp! Are you fed up to here with Black, Chicano and Yang criminals who break into lockers, and steal your clothes and wallets? Join the Klan Youth Corps!" In order to appeal to mainstream America, Duke went so far as to have his nose done and had his hair styled as if he were a blond John F. Kennedy. He tried to distance himself from his Klan activities and denied that he was the person pictured on a college campus wearing a swastika band on his Nazi uniform. In 1980, Duke announced that he was going to run for President.[18] He never actually ran. In 1990, he ran for the U.S. Senate in Louisiana, campaigning on such issues as affirmative action, immigration, crime, drugs, welfare, and AIDS—perfect subjects to gain popularity in an economically strained period. Duke lost the election but gained 45 percent of the total vote and 65 percent of the white vote. Those are significant numbers.[19]

In 1981, there were over 10,000 Klan members, while over 100,000 nonmembers supported their efforts. "Klaverns were found in half the states and in all branches of the Armed Forces." But membership in the Klan has decreased drastically. In the 1990s, the Klan population is estimated at 4,000. According to Thomas Halpern, Assistant Director of the Fact Finding Department of the Anti-Defamation League, "In

1993, the Invisible Empire Knights of the KKK (the largest faction) reached a settlement with civil rights marchers who had sued the Klan for attacks on the marchers by Klan members and sympathizers in Georgia in 1987. The settlement involved a payment by the Klan to the marchers of $37,500. But more importantly, as a consequence of the settlement, the Invisible Empire faction has dissolved. (A small splinter group has attempted to reorganize under a new name, but it shows no sign of genuine strength so far.) This was a real victory against the KKK in America."[20]

A significant word in the above report is "reorganize." Hate groups will always exist. They may use a different name or they may be branches of the newer hate groups like the Aryan Nation or the Skinheads. As long as one group will not take the time to understand other groups that are thought to be inferior, they will not disappear.

## Tom Metzger and the White Aryan Resistance

Tom Metzger, the creator and leader of the White Aryan Resistance (another hate group with a large appeal to young white males), is another example of a media manipulator. He would appear on television in a business suit and speak about how he loved his white race and would do anything to preserve it. He even hosted his own cable show, *Race and Reason*, on which people were free to say anything they wanted about "stupid niggers and sneaky Jews." At present Metzger is serving time in prison for the murder of a member of the Resistance who wanted to leave the group. However, his son carries on his work, making frequent television appearances dressed like a young computer corporation executive and addressing his audience in a soft, articulate voice.

## Aryan Nation

Aryan Nation conducts world congresses every summer in Hayden Lake, Idaho, at which time classes in terrorism, guerrilla warfare, and general hate mongering are taught. Through "Aryan Nation Newsletter," "Calling Our Nation," and "The Way," its three publications, Aryan Nation reaches across America. "The Way" is distributed in prisons where the hate group enlists many of its members. But because so much of the material is inflammatory, prison officials in many states have forbidden its distribution.

In several small towns in Ohio, fliers left on lawns had slogans on them such as "Hitler was right." The fliers were identified as being the work of the Aryan Nation and included a phone number for those who wanted more information about the "militant white separatist Christian organization." No legal action was taken because Ohio law "makes hateful expression illegal only if it directly incites lawbreaking or directly causes it."[21]

Hate groups that use "church" names give the group members some feeling of righteousness because they are told that the pain they inflict on minorities has God's sanction. The Identity Church, a hate group that passes itself off as a religion, emerged in the late seventies. But its roots go back to Anglo-Israelism, a nineteenth-century philosophy that claims the Anglo-Saxons are the true descendants of the ten lost tribes of Israel. They also state that England and the United States are the lands where the chosen people shall find the fulfillment of the Bible. Today, the Identity Church considers all minorities to be inferior.

## Skinheads

Another hate group that has wreaked its share of havoc was actually born in England in about 1970. The Skinheads (their name is derived from their shaved scalps) come across as "tough, patriotic, anti-immigrant, working class" young thugs, ranging in age from thirteen to twenty-five. They are a dangerous threat because after years of moderate activity, these neo-Nazis seem to be on the rise once again. Disguised as what most people believe are misguided youth who are into alcohol, drugs, and hard-driving music (though drinking, using drugs, and liking that type of music are not necessarily restricted to neo-Nazis), the Skinheads are the most violent of the white supremacist groups. They inflict pain on such defenseless people as a homeless black man in Alabama, a gay white man and a lesbian black in Oregon, a black Olympic athlete in Oberhof, Germany, and a fifteen-year-old Vietnamese boy who begged for forgiveness for coming to this country.

The Skinheads are not a unified organization, however. They are loosely connected units with a membership totaling

Skinheads, like the ones shown here, pose a dangerous threat to society. The activities of this group of neo-Nazis seem to be on the rise throughout America.

about thirty-five hundred. They serve as "front-line warriors" for groups like the KKK and Aryan Nations in about forty states and in some European countries.[22]

Are the hate groups worth worrying about? Are they a threat? Even one bias attack is worth worrying about. One bias attack is a threat. Members can dress the way they want; they can listen to any music of their liking; they can enjoy all their rights and privileges. But once they attempt—not even commit—violence, the law must intervene. It is a matter of constitutionality in twenty-eight states and should be in all states. Once a hate crime is committed, the law has the right and power to inflict a more severe punishment.[23]

## Splinter Groups

Splinter groups pop up in every community. For example, on the morning of October 5, 1993, a Molotov cocktail (a type of bomb made by putting a flammable liquid and a rag wick in a glass bottle) was tossed into the home of Jimmie Yee, a Chinese-American city councilman of Sacramento, California. Soon after, the police and several television stations were called by a man who identified himself as a member of the Aryan Liberation Front. He announced that he was responsible for the firebombing and also for attacking the Japanese American Citizens League, the Sacramento branch of the NAACP, and a local synagogue. This splinter group was a surprise because Sacramento is 40 percent minority and hardly a hotbed of racial turmoil.[24]

Hate groups like the skinheads shown here are indeed worth worrying about. Only twenty-eight of our fifty states have laws against the violence of hate crimes.

## Black Racism

For some people, the idea of a black racist is incomprehensible, since blacks are the victims of racism. Until recently, the question of how blacks view whites has been largely unexplored. But new work by pollsters, sociologists, and political scientists has uncovered evidence of specific negative attitudes that black people harbor toward white people.

A study published by the National Conference of Christians and Jews found that blacks feel that whites think themselves superior, and that "they do not want to share power and wealth with nonwhites." The poll also found that blacks' negative feelings toward whites is far greater than that of other minorities, such as Latinos and Asian Americans.

Today's social and economic conditions tend to ensure that black resentment of whites will not diminish soon. According to the U.S. census, poverty rates among blacks remain high and blacks continue to be the most segregated group. Whether it is the result of whites making blacks unwelcome, or of declining faith in integration among some blacks, black Americans and white Americans live apart. Those who want to reach out to each other sometimes are labeled as Uncle Toms or bleeding heart liberals, or jeered at for "acting white."[25]

## Louis Farrakhan and the Nation of Islam

The Nation of Islam was founded in Detroit in 1930 by Wallace D. Ford because many African Americans rejected

Christianity as a "slave" religion and were looking for their ethnic heritage and pride. Ford was replaced about five years later by Elijah Poole, renamed Elijah Muhammed. He developed the Nation of Islam into an African-American nationalist business and religious empire. In 1975, Elijah Muhammed was succeeded by his son Wallace, who shifted the movement away from African-American nationalism to a more orthodox Islam; he also gave it a new name. Louis Farrakhan, who joined the nation of Islam in 1955, and rose to become one of several Nation of Islam leaders by 1975, resisted Wallace's direction because he wanted to adhere to Elijah Muhammed's original concept. Eventually, Farrakhan became the leader of an offshoot of the Nation of Islam, the Lost-Found Nation of Islam, and took Elijah Muhammed's view of nationalism even further. Some consider Farrakhan a racist.

The Nation of Islam has mosques or temples in 120 cities. Though exact figures cannot be determined, membership is estimated at from 30,000 to 200,000. All ministers are appointed by Farrakhan. Male members earn their way up in the Fruit of Islam. These are young members of Nation of Islam—mostly bodyguards. They are given military-style stripes and ranks but do not carry weapons. In addition to classes to learn about the history of African-American men, proper discipline, and proper dress, men also sell the Nation of Islam's newspaper, *The Final Call.* The more they sell, the greater their chance of rising up the ranks of the organization.[26]

Farrakhan's message to his members and potential new recruits is one of African-American self-determination, but it is often buried in words that are sometimes as hateful as those used by white racist groups.

According to Michael Meyers, executive director of the New York Civil Rights Coalition and former assistant director of the NAACP, "Louis Farrakhan is an unadulterated race man . . . who believes in the partitioning of America into black and white sections, and a black racist who says that having dark skin makes one better than Caucasians. . . . Farrakhan is infatuated with the power of the media to carry his fiery, extremist message . . . that, for him, reinforces in his black faithful a belief in the white power structure's fear of the free 'authentic' voice of the black masses."[27]

When he was labeled as anti-Semitic, Farrakhan reacted by making such statements as: Judaism is a "gutter religion," and Hitler was "wickedly great." One member of the Fruit of Islam acknowledges that Farrakhan's fury at whites is unrelenting. Farrakhan's preaching reinforces his resentment. He has said, "I don't think there's anything wrong with saying I hate them. They have caused me harm over and over, and I wish they were dead."[28]

Farrakhan claimed that AIDS was created by the American government to eliminate the population of central Africa. To remedy the suffering of black Americans, he told *People* magazine, the country must raise them up from being the underclass. If not, it must pay them reparations, free all blacks from American prisons, and use the money previously spent on keeping these men and women in prisons to create a homeland for them in Africa. He also claimed that black-on-black violence is advantageous to whites because it provides organ donations. "When a rich white person needs a kidney or a heart, get us a nigger," said Farrakhan, who is paid in the neighborhood of $15,000 to $20,000 per lecture,[29] to a nearly all male audience of 6000 at an antiviolence rally at the University of Toledo, "When you're killing each other, they can't wait for you to die. You've become good for parts."[30]

In March 1994, he addressed a crowd of 9000 men in Washington, D.C., to encourage them to stop the killing of blacks by blacks. Women were not allowed to attend because Farrakhan did not think they were as directly involved in the problem. "We are participating in our own destruction. . . . It is time for we [*sic*] as men to sit together and carve out a future for our people." To suggest that his approach had taken a different turn, Farrakhan added, "I want to go to the core of you, not the color of you. You have a duty to the Creator."[31]

Though this speech did not focus on anti-Semitism, those who attended noticed that along with the posters, T-shirts, and videotapes that were sold in the armory vestibule, were books with titles like *The Jewish Onslaught, Jews and their Lies,* and *The Secret Relationship between Blacks and Jews.* The speech came soon after Farrakhan demoted Khalid Abdul Muhammad, one of his closest associates, for making anti-Semitic remarks while speaking at Kean College of New Jersey on November 29, 1993.[32]

Even with the messages from the new Nation of Islam and other African-American nationalists, America has experienced no episodes of large-scale, well-coordinated attacks by blacks against whites. But individual attacks—like the beating of Reginald Denny during the Los Angeles riots, and the attack by Colin Ferguson, the gunman who killed whites and Asians on the Long Island Railroad commuter train in New York—demonstrate that black racism, just like white racism, can maim and kill people as well as poison the atmosphere.

*chapter*

# 4

# Institutional Racism

From the time you were a child until now you have probably spent more than 15,000 hours watching television. That's 5000 hours more than the time you will spend doing homework from elementary school through high school.[1]

## Racism and Television

For more than forty years television has been the centerpiece in American homes, and the prime source of information for most Americans. There are more than 96 million households in America, and 98 percent of those homes have a television set. In fact, more homes have TV sets than have indoor plumbing.[2]

Now, imagine the influence of such a tremendous cultural force over more than 250 million lives. For the first twenty-five years of its existence, few African Americans or Asian

Americans appeared on the television screen. The exceptions were those who appeared as domestic help in situation comedies, or those who made special guest appearances on variety or dramatic shows. Nat King Cole, the father of singer Natalie Cole, did have his own half-hour variety show, but he had very little decision-making power. Most of his guests were white entertainers, and he had difficulty getting black entertainers to perform on his show. There were no black newscasters, political commentators, or weatherpeople, and an Asian-American newscaster was unheard of. How could this be possible? The absence of people of color on television is an example of institutional racism. This kind of racism goes beyond individual thoughts and actions. Social institutions, such as family, church, school, business, and government create patterns of racial injustice and inequality, and reinforce racist ideas. People involved in these institutions may not even be aware that they are participating in racism.

Twenty-five years ago, the television screen reflected what was considered to be the average television household. While decision makers in the television industry at that time may have seemed to be deliberately discriminating against people of color, racism was so deeply imbedded in the industry that few even considered that what was seen on television might not have been realistic. Furthermore, since there were no people of color in the television industry who had any power to make decisions, the subject of the lack of African Americans or Asian Americans on television wasn't even addressed.

What you're used to seeing on television now is a more accurate reflection of American society, one that took years of protest and legal maneuvers to accomplish. But there are those who would argue that television still does not reflect society accurately. Some of this problem is being resolved through the introduction of cable television to American homes. Cable increases the choice of stations from about fifteen stations to more than fifty, with programming reflecting the diversity in all of America.

## Racism and the School System

Another American institution having a profound effect on children and teenagers is, of course, our school system. Efforts to successfully integrate our schools were underway by 1954, to conform with *Brown* v. *Board of Education of Topeka, Kansas*, the Supreme Court case that declared segregation illegal. By the 1970s, however, the educational system was cited for instances of institutional racism.

After a thorough study of classroom materials, it was concluded that textbooks rarely represented minority groups. As children were learning their ABCs, they might also be learning that there were no African-American mothers and fathers or "Dick and Janes." In case after case, the textbooks were not reflecting the actual experiences of the students who were attending school. The books were changed.

Further social and political changes brought about changes in the curriculum that reflected a broader understanding of our culture. In contrast to the idea of the United

*Brown* v. *Board of Education of Topeka, Kansas,* the Supreme Court case that declared segregation in our public schools illegal, was not implemented without dramatic moments. This officer of the national guard stands watch over Central High School in Little Rock, Arkansas.

States as a melting pot, which promised to erase ethnic and group differences, children now learn that differences among groups are a national resource rather than a problem to be solved. It is also now recognized that the common culture of the United States is multicultural. According to Catherine R. Stimpson of Rutgers University, "we must listen to a 'diversity of voices' in order to understand our culture, past and present."[3] This point of view has led to major revisions in what children are taught and what they read in school.

As you know, school systems are being reviewed constantly, always with the view to making education better. It is the role of the school systems to prepare students to become productive members of society. It is also their role to teach students how to live and work together, and how to respect each other's rights. In an effort to ensure that schools were not teaching racism, studies were undertaken to determine if schoolchildren chose their playmates based on race. The reason for these studies was that teachers and professional sociologists as well as psychologists believed students did, in fact, select playmates along racial lines. If this was in fact the case, they reasoned, what good would all the changes in curriculum be if children still believed that some were better than others because of the color of their skin.

Surprisingly, studies undertaken both in America and in England revealed the same conclusion: for the most part, children *do not* base their choice of playmates along racial lines.[4] Depending on the situation, children may choose friends based on how smart they are, how well they play kickball, who brings the best sandwiches from home, or who is the silliest. The research was based not only on what children said, but on what they did. Some children did say they didn't like African Americans or Asian Americans as a group because of what they might have heard at home or seen on television. But their actions proved that on an individual basis, what they said had little to do with their choice of friends.

Also, the research pointed out that over the past twenty years, schools as an institution have been very successful in teaching children that it is wrong to judge people based on the color of their skin.[5] In fact, many of the children who were interviewed said that they knew it was wrong not to like someone just because he or she was different. This is promising news, since the children will grow to be adults, and the adults will be responsible for making social policy that abolishes racism.

## Racism and the Workplace

The American workplace also shows evidence of institutional racism. While public service jobs are bound by government rules to promote equal opportunity and prohibit overt racist acts, in private business, progress in abolishing racism comes more slowly. According to the Equal Employment Opportunity Commission, complaints of racially motivated discrimination or harrassment increased over 8.5 percent from 1992 to 1993, to a total of 125,217 complaints.[6] Federal authorities and management experts say that much of the reason for the increase in complaints is because more private companies are hiring minorities, including women. But this may be resented by white males, who worry about job security during uneven financial times and then take this frustrating set of circumstances out on minority workers. According to Mildred Saunders, a New York–based consultant on equal employment matters, "whenever people are different and fewer jobs are available because of the economy, these kinds of issues are commonplace."[7] Paul C. Sprenger, an attorney who specializes in employment litigation, points out that this kind of racism is "second generation." He said the first generation of lawsuits was to get people hired. He added, "now we have to make sure that people are treated fairly."[8] In fact, the federal government has initiated lawsuits recently (July, 1993) seeking fairness in who gets fired first when a company is downsizing.[9]

## *Racism and Health Care*

One of the major problems all Americans face is the quality of their health care. In the 1994 congressional year, health care reform, as well as universal coverage, was a priority for Congress and it was eager to get some legislation passed. One of the known inequities in health care is that the service provided is only as good as the medical insurance the patient has. But recently, two studies appearing in the *Journal of the American Medical Association* suggest that treatment may vary with the race of the patient, and not with the kind of insurance the patient does or does not have.[10] This is another example of institutional racism.

75

In the first study the quality of care given to 9,932 Medicare patients was evaluated. The patients were treated at 297 hospitals in 30 cities and towns in 5 states. According to Dr. Katherine L. Kahn, the study's lead author: "Within each type of hospital, patients who were black or from poor neighborhoods got less care."[11]

In the second study, it was found that in Veterans Administration hospitals, blacks who suffered heart attacks received less medical treatment than whites, even though both groups had identical coverage. Dr. Eric Peterson, a Duke University Medical Center cardiologist, helped to conduct the studies. He said the evidence seems to be that the disparity in treatment points to racism as a factor when patients have the same health coverage and socioeconomic backgrounds.

As a result of these reports, medical experts said the nation's doctors and nurses have to take a step back and reflect on the quality of care they provide. Doctors and nurses are sworn to save lives, and it should make no difference to them if the patient they are saving is black or white. If more studies are completed with the same results, the nation's hospitals, as well as the government, will have to be more aggressive in ensuring equality of medical treatment. Doctors and nurses will have to do more than "step back and reflect" on the care they presently give.

The words of Alexis de Tocqueville, the French historian who wrote *Democracy in America*, come back to remind us that it is no easy thing to combat racism. In reference to slavery, he said that in the ancient empires of Rome and Egypt

AM I NOT A MAN AND A BROTHER?

Alexis de Tocqueville, a French historian, predicted that changing the law to abolish slavery would be easy compared to changing people's minds about slavery. His prediction seems to have come true. Over thirty years after the Civil Rights Act of 1964, we are still faced with many problems that can be traced back to the days of slavery.

the hardest thing that had to be done to abolish slavery was to change the law. But in the United States, he predicted that changing the law to abolish slavery would be easy compared to changing people's minds about slavery and racism.

But people's minds can be changed. Studies have proven that when people are presented with the facts of an issue on a one-to-one basis, minds can be changed.[12] Additionally, it has been found that the positions white people take on a number of social issues dealing with black people are not the same across the board.[13] A person can support equal housing for blacks as well as increased spending for more job training for blacks. But that same person may be totally against any policies dealing with affirmative action for blacks or any other minority group. What this should help you to see is that racism may not always be the reason why a person formulates a particular opinion on social policy having to do with blacks and other minorities.

So, while we may find that discussions of social policy issues are not always based on racist attitudes, we may also be surprised at the tremendous progress schools have made in abolishing racism. In other areas, however, such as in private business, and recently in medical care, more progress needs to be made.

# Racism Today

In order to understand what racism today is all about, we must briefly review the results of the 1964 Civil Rights Act. At that time, the Act was perceived as the high point of the civil rights movement, which had begun more than two hundred years before.

## Affirmative Action

Under Title VII of the Civil Rights Act, discrimination in employment based on race, religion, gender, or national origin was banned. It seemed as if employment opportunities would now be opened for everyone. But, it was also obvious that many people who could benefit from this law did not have the necessary skills or experience to qualify for these positions. Furthermore, many of the employers who had to follow the law found reasons, based on their own racist

President Lyndon Baines Johnson signed the 1968 Civil Rights Bill in an effort to abolish discrimination based on race. Over twenty-five years later, we are still struggling to create racial equality in society.

beliefs, not to hire African Americans. Therefore, a policy of "affirmative action"—steps taken to have a racially balanced workforce—was initiated. Under this policy, preferential treatment would be given to African Americans and other minorities in securing jobs and subsequent promotions, even though they might lack the required experience or skills. After all, it was argued, you couldn't expect people who had never held these jobs because of discrimination, racial or otherwise, to compete on the same basis as those already in that workforce.

In order to make sure that this policy was followed, the Fair Employment Practices Committee, originally begun in 1941 to ensure that defense plants would hire African Americans, had its authority enhanced. Its name was also changed to the Equal Employment Opportunities Commission (EEOC). Today, the EEOC is responsible for thousands of lawsuits against employers who do not observe all the Title VII laws.

Were these actions successful? By all measures, the workforce has become a more accurate reflection of the population, especially in government or civil service jobs. And while the African-American population doubled between 1950 and 1990, the number of African Americans who earned more than $50,000 in inflation-adjusted dollars, went from 1 in 17 to 1 in 7 in 1989.[1]

Affirmative action policies were created to abolish discriminatory hiring practices based on race. After more than twenty years, those same policies have worked to create a new kind of racism. The so-called new racists are longtime supporters of civil rights, but they are also aware that African Americans who have been very successful in the workforce were given "preferential treatment." African Americans, according to new racists, are like commodities. You need to have a certain amount of them to meet government rules, and you have to be careful about what you say about their work or you might be subject to a lawsuit.

According to Ellis Cose, a contributing editor at *Newsweek* magazine and the author of *The Rage of a Privileged Class*, however, many of the black people he interviewed for his book felt that they carried an extra burden: proving themselves to their white counterparts in the workforce. He says that almost all the people he talked to "touched on the great amount of energy they have to spend just making white people comfortable around them."[2]

These results show that the government has to be careful about the policies it uses to help abolish racism. Policies can have unexpected and unwanted results.

## Reverse Discrimination

One unexpected result in the pursuit of affirmative action was the perception among white people that they might lose their jobs or not be promoted because their employers have to give more favored treatment to a black person who wanted the same job or promotion. This fear came to be known as reverse discrimination. An example of this can be found in the case of Allan Bakke.[3] He sued the University of California in 1978 because his application to its medical school was rejected. Bakke claimed he was rejected in favor of a black candidate who did not have the same marks or credentials as he did. Bakke said he was rejected because he was white, and that was just as discriminatory as rejecting someone because he is black. In this case, the court ruled that colleges and universities have the right to decide what the composition of its student bodies would be. However, they did direct the medical school to admit Mr. Bakke. In a recent case against the University of Texas Law School, three white students were rejected in favor of black students. The court ordered the three white students admitted to the law school. In this case the court decided that the policy of the law school was discriminatory.

It would seem reasonable that some special treatment is due because of all the years blacks weren't admitted to medical schools or law schools in any great numbers, or hired or promoted. Yet, in this area, white Americans seem to be firm. They don't feel they have to be held accountable for past discrimination. And as was shown in research discussed in a previous chapter, white Americans can change their minds on other social policies when presented with a good argument, but on the policy of "affirmative action," there is sometimes very little flexibility.

## Resegregation on College Campuses

Evidence of a new kind of racism is appearing on college campuses. Colleges and universities made great efforts to diversify their student populations through affirmative action policies similar to those undertaken in the workplace. Yet today segregation on campus has become almost a way of life.

*U.S. News & World Report* surveyed 550 student editors about race relations on campus. Nine out of ten editors at larger schools reported that self-segregation by blacks and other minority students on campus was common.[4] The problem is that when too many black, white, and other minority students live apart, play apart, and eat apart, they also grow apart. According to one student editor at Iowa State University: "We have a campus of 25,000 students and there is no mixing across cultural or racial lines."[5] The editor pointed out that after a major racial skirmish on campus a rally for cultural unity was held. Unfortunately, the editor noted, "all the blacks clustered together and all the whites clustered together."[6] At the end of the twentieth century segregated campuses would seem to be the exact opposite of what affirmative action policies on college campuses were supposed to achieve.

Some social scientists now believe that the resegregated campus can be traced to what has happened in the public schools. In the Northeast and Midwest, the city schools have gone from populations of mostly white to overwhelmingly African-American and other minority students. For black and other minority parents this situation is not as bad as it seems. The nation's effort to integrate schools, based on the *Brown* v. *Board of Education* ruling in 1954, has come under attack. Some black scholars believe that the rationale behind the ruling was racist. For these scholars, segregation conferred on black children the stigma of inferiority, and the only way to change that was by integrating black students into white schools. This meant that black children couldn't succeed on their own, and, therefore, many blacks see integration as a white plot to undermine racial pride. It isn't surprising then that black parents would support the all-black academies that have been instituted or discussed in such cities as Chicago, New York, and Miami as a better way of instilling black self-esteem, and as a much better alternative to busing black children to largely white suburban schools. If these beliefs are prevalent at the public and high school level, then segregated campuses at college do not seem so unusual.[7]

Other instances that have strained relations between African-American and minority students and nonminority students have to do with the areas of ethnic studies and the right of student groups to listen to certain controversial speakers. In particular, at the City College campus in New York, the head of the African-American studies department, Dr. Leonard Jeffries, has been accused of being anti-Semitic because he claims that the Jews were responsible for slavery and for keeping blacks out of the movies or in movie roles that reinforced the stereotype of blacks being inferior. Dr. Jefferies also presents some theories about skin color and the origin of civilization that, it is claimed by other educators in the same field, have no basis in fact. But if anyone questions Jeffries' curriculum or his findings, he or she will often be attacked as a racist. John Hope Franklin, former head of the history

This civil rights march on Washington, D.C. in 1963 was at the beginning
of the trend toward racial equality in this country.

departments at Brooklyn College in New York City and at the University of Chicago, is called "the dean of black historians in America today."[8] He warns that a black scholar must "understand the difference between hard-hitting advocacy on the one hand and the highest standards of scholarship on the other."[9] If Dr. Jeffries is perceived as going too far, he could cause further dissension on campus and could discredit the entire legitimate field of African-American studies.

Another divisive action taken by some black student groups is to invite guest speakers who, by the nature of what they say, do more harm than good to black-white relations. The Rev. Louis Farrakhan and other members of the Nation of Islam, for example, have often been invited to speak on campuses. Nonminority students who wish to hear him are sometimes excluded. Because what he and other members of his group say has been termed "antiwhite," "antigay," "anti-Semitic," and "anti-Catholic," his presence has caused great discomfort among many groups on campus.[10] You can see how these problems can be further heightened when campuses are self-segregated and there is very little or no communication between groups.

## Multicultural vs. Ethnocentric Curriculums

Since the beginning of the civil rights movement, the trend has been to make the institutions in America more representative of the diversity of the people they serve. An individual's cultural heritage is now emphasized in an effort to increase his or her pride and self-esteem. As a result of the success of the civil rights movement, the women's liberation movement, movements focusing on such groups as the physically and mentally disabled, and the gay rights movement seek to include everyone as full participants in and beneficiaries of American society. This trend has also prompted historians and educators to recognize contributions from all groups and incorporate these findings into what is being taught in our schools.

Some think the multicultural approach to education diminishes traditional educational teachings, which are based on Western European culture. Others think that the Western European tradition excludes diverse groups because its contributors are largely white, of European background, and male. Still others are proponents of an ethnocentric approach to education. This last approach may present a problem, since it would seem to divide even further what should be a more cohesive point-of-view.

"Africa is the mother of Western civilization . . . " This statement was made by Professor Asa Hilliard, an African-American psychologist at Georgia State University.[11] He wrote "African-American Baseline Essays," which was incorporated into the curriculum of several large public education systems in America in the late 1980s. According to Professor Hilliard, and other educators, the emphasis on "white, racist" curriculum did not include the contributions of minorities, most notably blacks.

In response to this lack, the Afrocentric curriculum was developed. But rather than acknowledge Western European responsible for various parts of the curriculum, claim that the credit for *all* of western civilization should go to Africa. They base this idea on the theory that Egypt was a black African country and was the real source of the science and philosophy western historians attribute to Greece. Professor Hilliard also credits Africans with the invention of birth control and carbon steel. This kind of curriculum—where *everything* is viewed from the perspective of Africa, rather than striving for balance—can do more damage than good, further separating blacks and whites.

In the long run, there is only one way we'll be able to measure the success of these different curriculum approaches. The one that will produce citizens who can ably function in the highly technical, computerized, and globally interactive frontier of the twenty-first century will come out ahead.

## Political Correctness and Racism

The multiculturalism approach has had a tremendous impact on college campuses in one particular area. In an effort to be more sensitive to the diverse groups on campus, efforts have been made to restrict racist and sexist speech. This is called being "politically correct." At the base of this speech code is the concept that a person who is offended or hurt has a right to say what language is offending or hurting him or her. He or she can even bring charges against the person who is using the offensive language, when that person may not realize that the language is offensive. The political correctness movement also demands behavioral reforms by "white American males," calling them "oppressors." Everyone else on campus is labeled oppressed.

Many campuses have speech code committees that develop speech codes and that determine whether a particular word is politically incorrect. Some people think this type of monitoring of students' as well as teachers' speech is pure censorship, and that it limits a person from speaking the truth because it might hurt someone.

The pros and cons of political correctness were discussed in a debate on the television program *Firing Line* on December 6, 1993. The proposition was that political correctness was a menace and a bore. One of the participants in the debate was Linda S. Greene, an African-American professor at the University of Wisconsin Law School. While her original intention was to defend the policy of political correctness, what she said instead was far more interesting: "What we need to do is not focus on calling each other racist or sexist, but instead try to understand how historical racism has affected our lives . . . "[12] Professor Greene then went on to explain that politically correct committees are more interested in defining victims than they are in attacking racism.

The political correctness movement, however well intentioned, may indeed be another example of how words can do damage, by confusing what should be focused upon: transforming our society in such a way that the word *racism* and the actions behind it are eliminated.

## The Media and Racism

Racism on college campuses, multicultural education, affirmative action policy, the political correctness movement, are all hot topics that receive heavy coverage by the media. The media thus may have an influential role in promoting or discouraging twenty-first century racism.

Television (including cable), radio, and print media provides us with information about our neighborhood, our country, and the world at breakneck speed. Because of the nature of communication technology, we were able to see Nelson Mandela inaugurated as president of South Africa as it happened. Similarly, we were able to witness the devastating Los Angeles riots of 1992. Both of these events had historical meaning not only for African Americans, but for all Americans.

When media works well, it is the miracle of the ages. But we must also acknowledge that decisions to cover a particular event may be influenced by what news the media executives feel will attract the most viewers or readers. Sometimes this results in coverage of more sensational events, such as protests or riots, or coverage of certain people or groups who are intent on creating division, fear, and hatred. Meanwhile, an event involving more positive human endeavors, such as people working together to build a community park, or the graduation of a class of students who have successfully overcome hardships, receives much less coverage, or no coverage at all. Sometimes positive events receive coverage by special programming, as if these events don't happen every day.

Let's look at an example. When the 1992 trial of four policemen accused of beating Rodney King, a black man, resulted in mostly not guilty decisions, people living in downtown Los Angeles rioted in protest. Television coverage was immediate. We could see people looting, throwing bricks into windows, and beating innocent drivers who happened into the area. Few people will ever forget the image of the white truck driver, Reginald Denny, who was dragged out of his truck and beaten by some black rioters. But how many people remember that the person who helped Mr. Denny and dispersed the crowd was a black minister who was in considerable danger himself. While everyone would agree that the Los Angeles riots were devastating, it seemed that media coverage was mostly geared to seeking out examples of outrageous criminal behavior, which did even more damage to black/white relations. When the policemen were tried again under a federal indictment, it was rumored that many leaders of the black community threatened a repeat of the riots in Los Angeles if there were no convictions of the white policemen this time. Could these threats, coupled with the memory of the previous riots, have had an effect on the second jury, which did convict some of the policemen? We do not know. But we can see that the actions taken by the media may have done more to further racism than it did to overcome it.

Just as the media can manipulate what news will be presented to American readers, listeners, and viewers, certain people or groups can manipulate the media. In fact, the re-emergence of certain hate groups such as the Ku Klux Klan and Nazi sympathizers may be due to how much coverage these groups get on talk shows as well as news broadcasts, over and above the real influence they have. These groups are students of the media. They know that if they say they want to get rid of all black people, all Jewish people, and all people who aren't "pure white," they'll make headlines. The more racial hatred they spout, the more threatening they seem, and the more likely you will see them on television.

Aryan Nations, Knights of the Ku Klux Klan, and the National Association for the Advancement of White People represent the extreme of racism today. They use the media well. As long as there are otherwise reasonable people who may have a political gripe with how the government runs such programs as affirmative action, there will be a place for hate groups. The best way to prevent hate groups from making any of their goals a reality is to recognize the way they operate, and constantly present them with the truth everytime the opportunity presents itself.

# 6

# Next Steps

On May 10, 1994, Cable News Network (CNN) revealed the results of a poll it took together with *The Los Angeles Times* to assess what damage was done to white/black relations, two years after the Los Angeles riots. The poll revealed that 78 percent of the people surveyed thought America hadn't come anywhere near abolishing racism.[1] After all the efforts of the civil rights movement, could it be true that an overwhelming majority of people think nothing has really changed? Or is the media manipulating information again?

If you were not satisfied with these findings, what could you do? As a concerned citizen, you could find out more about the survey. You could phone CNN or *The Los Angeles Times* and ask for a copy of the survey or its major findings. You could find out the size of the group interviewed. What was its racial makeup? What kind of people (professionals, working class, and so on) were interviewed? Were they old or young? What was their income? What was the average level of education? How did the group answer other questions? You may not be a research scientist, but if the majority of the people interviewed were victims of racism, their answers might tend to lead to the conclusion that racism will never be abolished. That's just one way of looking at the issue.

While no one pretends that racism will be completely abolished, perhaps government efforts to enforce nondiscriminatory policies in employment, education, and housing are not enough. Or perhaps success in abolishing racism should not be measured by the success or failure of government policy alone. As current research shows, when people are judged on an individual basis and not as a group with certain racial characteristics, previously held opinions can and do change.

That's where you come in. You are an individual. And you can change the mind of other individuals. You can do it by knowing the facts of history and the nature of human behavior. You can do it by realizing that human beings aren't perfect and that fear and ignorance are the biggest barriers to change for anyone.

You can help to abolish racism by not being taken in with arguments that bypass the facts and concentrate on name calling. When you hear a statement on such as "The white race is superior," or "All civilization originated with the black race," ask the person who made the statement on what facts he or she is basing his or her point of view. Don't just blindly accept those facts. Confirm the statements and facts through other reliable sources.

You can help to abolish racism by understanding how language is being used. The concept of races of people was created by scientists to classify differences among human beings. You know that the three-race theory of classification is not accurate, as it once was proclaimed, because there are too many variations within any race. You also know that dividing people by race doesn't "prove" anything unless you like to count numbers for the U.S. Census Bureau, or for the U.S. Statistical Abstract. Statistics can be manipulated to demonstrate any point anyone wants to make. If the statistics are repeated often enough, people will come to believe them. That's why you must always ask from where statistics being used come. You must always ask yourself why special interest groups might exaggerate figures.

Another way to eliminate racism is to make every effort to recognize and appreciate *all* cultures. Cultural pride is important, but if progress is to be made in eliminating racism on a one-to-one basis, then it is important to recognize and appreciate what other races have to offer. It is only when you declare your own group superior to other groups, and then keep groups apart, that the seeds of racism can be planted and grow.

Yet another way is by emulating those who are setting a positive example for you, such as members of your family, your religious leaders, your friends, or your teachers. Examine the lives of those who have made significant contributions to

Jesse Jackson is one of many African Americans who has made significant contributions to his culture. In his own way, he has influenced the course of history.

your own culture or to society in general. Here are some people who have influenced African-American history:

- **Mary Mcleod Bethone** opened a school for African-American girls in 1904 in Florida. Her school went on to become a four-year college.

- **W. E. B. DuBois** created the NAACP in 1909 because he was so infuriated that as the twentieth century was beginning, African Americans still were forced to use separate restrooms, water fountains, waiting rooms, and even libraries.

- **Jesse Jackson**, one of Dr. King's followers, created "Operation Breadbasket" in 1968. It is an organization that was able to find employment for thousands of African Americans and to assist others in opening businesses of their own. In 1984 he registered more than two million African Americans to be able to vote.

- **Martin Luther King, Jr.**, led a non-violent band of devoted followers, both black and white, in the fight for political, social, and economic equality that launched the civil rights movement of the 1960s.

- **Malcolm X**, though considered too militant by some, during the 1960s taught all Americans about black pride, dignity, and self-esteem.

- **Thurgood Marshall**, was the Supreme Court Justice who helped rid America of the "separate-but equal" law by arguing in *Brown* v. *Board of Education of Topeka, Kansas*

Malcolm X taught all Americans about being proud of who you are, having dignity, and having self-esteem. These are important things for everyone to remember, regardless of their race.

that all children were entitled to an equal education as granted by the Constitution's Fourteenth Amendment.

- **Sojourner Truth** was a former slave who fought for and gained her freedom. She went on to fight for the rights of all African Americans.

- **Booker T. Washington** became president of Tuskegee Institute in 1881. He urged his students to become proficient at a trade or profession so that they could earn respectable wages and develop into more responsible people.

- **Ida B. Wells-Barnett** was a journalist whose lifelong fight against discrimination began at age sixteen. She was one of the founders of the NAACP.

One of the things that all these important people share is schooling. Their zeal to free their own people from the shackles of bigotry developed because they were educated. They learned to think and to criticize constructively. Through these abilities, they sought the best for themselves and their, or perhaps all, people. Let them set that example for you.

Finally, the best asset you have is your youth. Your opinions are not so ingrained that you are not flexible enough to hear another person's point of view. Because you are young, chances are you are not so impatient that you would give up trying to abolish racism just because a person will not listen the first time.

So, when you hear or read statistics about racism that appear to be discouraging, get the facts. Understand why certain things are said by certain people. Ask yourself what their motivations are. Do they have a particular reason for their actions or remarks? Do they have the professional credentials that would lend authority to their statements?

Trust your education, your knowledge of history, and your sense of human behavior. Keep your perspective and try to put yourself in the other person's shoes. You'll do the right thing.

# Chapter Notes

## Introduction

1. Carl Sagan and Ann Dryan, *Shadows of Forgotten Ancestors: A Search for Who We Are* (New York: Random House, 1992), pp. 230–231.

2. Ibid., p. 235.

3. Bruce B. Svare, ed., *Hormones and Aggressive Behavior* (New York: Plenum Press, 1983), p. 359.

4. *Webster's New Twentieth Century Dictionary*, 2nd ed. (New York: The Publishers Guild, 1969), p. 181.

5. William Dudley and Charles Cozic, *Racism in America* (San Diego, Calif.: Greenhaven Press, Inc., 1991), p. 71.

6. Elaine Pascoe, *Racial Prejudice, Issues in American History* (New York: Franklin Watts, 1985), p. 9.

7. Abraham Lincoln, the Lincoln-Douglas Debates, 1858.

8. Senator John Franklin Miller, *The Congressional Record*, February 28, 1882.

9. Pascoe, p. 71.

## Chapter 1

1. *Webster's New Universal Unabridged Dictionary*, 2nd ed. (New York: Dorset & Baber, 1979), p. 1484.

2. Charles Darwin, *The Origin of the Species or The Preservation of Favored Races in the Struggle for Life* (New York: Avenel Books, 1979), p. 400.

3. Yehudi O. Webster, *The Racialization of America* (New York: St. Martin's Press, 1992), pp. 79–81.

4. Cynthia Crossen, *Tainted Truth: The Manipulation of Fact in America* (New York: Simon & Schuster, 1994), p. 16.

## Chapter 2

1. Bruno Leone, *Racism: Opposing Viewpoints* (St. Paul, Minn.: Greenhaven Press, 1986), p. 13.

2. Elaine Pascoe, *Racial Prejudice, Issues in American History* (New York: Franklin Watts, 1985), p. 5.

3. Ibid., p. 13.

4. Ibid., p. 6.

5. Ibid., p. 19.

6. Alexis de Tocqueville, *Democracy in America* (Garden City, N.Y.: Doubleday & Company, 1969), p. 341.

7. Anthony Lewis, "The Politics of Nativism," *The New York Times,* January 14, 1994, p. A29.

8. Ibid.

## Chapter 3

1. Bob Herbert, "Freedom Summer '94," *The New York Times,* June 26, 1994, p. 17.

2. Linda Yglesias, "Gov Hits Racism," *New York Daily News,* July 25, 1993, p. 6.

3. William A. Henry, III, "Pride and Prejudice," *Time,* February 28, 1994, p. 22.

4. Fred J. Cook, *The Ku Klux Klan* (New York: Julian Messner, 1980), pp. 14–20.

5. Patricia McKissack and Frederick McKissack, *The Civil Rights Movement in America* (Chicago: Childrens Press, 1987), pp. 39–40.

6. William Loren Katz, *The Invisible Empire* (Washington, D.C.: Open Hand Publishing, Inc., 1986), p. 28.

7. McKissack and McKissack, p. 48.

8. Ibid., pp. 60–74.

9. Katz, pp. 73–77.

10. Ibid., pp. 81–82.

11. Cook, pp. 62–63.

12. Katz, p. 131.

13. Sara Bullard, *Free at Last . . .* (New York: Oxford University Press, 1993), pp. 48–49.

14. Katz, p. 135.

15. Bullard, p. 60.

16. Ibid., p. 70.

17. Ibid., pp. 70–73.

18. Cook, pp. 143–152.

19. Irwin Suall and Thomas Halpern, *The KKK Today: A 1991 Status Report* (New York: Anti-Defamation League, 1991), p. 3.

20. Thomas Halpern, letter to author, May 12, 1994.

21. Anita McQueen, "Beachwood Hit by Neo-Nazi Leaflets," *Plain Dealer Reporter*, December 8, 1993, p. B2, Metro Section.

22. Irwin Suall and Thomas Halpern, *Young Nazi Killers* (New York: Anti-Defamation League, 1993), pp. 1–5.

23. Ibid., p. 28.

24. "White Supremacists Investigated in Four Firebombings in Sacramento," *The New York Times*, October 6, 1994, p. A18.

25. Steven A. Holmes, "Behind a Dark Mirror: Traditional Victims Give Vent to Racism," *The New York Times*, February 13, 1994, p. 4.

26. William A. Henry, III, "Pride and Prejudice," *Time*, February 28, 1994, p. 4.

27. Michael Meyers, "Time to Change the Politics of Hate," *New York Daily News*, February 22, 1994, p. 37.

28. Henry, pp. 26–27.

29. Shelby Steele, "How to Grow Extremists," *New York Times*, March 13, 1994, p. E17 (Op Ed).

30. *The New York Times*, May 2, 1994, p. 18, Sect. A.

31. Ibid.

32. Rene Sanchez, "Farrakhan Urges End to Violence: A Male Audience Told to Make Peace," *Washington Post*, March 22, 1994, p. B1.

## Chapter 4

1. John P. Robinson, "As We Like It," *American Demographics*, February 1993, p. 47.

2. James Twitchell, *Carnival Culture: The Trashing of Taste In America* (New York: Columbia University Press, 1992), p. 103.

3. William Dudley and Charles Cozic, *Racism in America* (San Diego, Calif.: Greenhaven Press, 1991), p. 202.

4. Barry Troyna and Richard Hatcher, *Racism in Children's Lives* (London: Routledge Press, 1992), pp. 24–29.

5. Ibid., pp. 198–200.

6. Michael Janofsky, *The Case Against Ford,"* The New York *Times*, June 20, 1993, p. 1, Sect. 3.

7. Ibid.

8. Ibid., p. 6.

9. Ibid., p. 5.

10. Sandra Blakeslee, "Poor and Black Patients Slighted," *The New York Times*, April 20, 1994, p. B9.

11. Ibid.

12. Paul M. Sniderman and Thomas Piazza, *The Scar of Race* (Cambridge, Mass.: Harvard University Press, 1993), p. 11.

13. Ibid.

## Chapter 5

1. William A. Henry, III, *In Defense of Elitism* (New York: Doubleday, 1994), p. 71.

2. Arnold Rampersad, "The Rage of the Privileged Class," *New York Times Book Review*, January 9, 1994, p. 6.

3. Andrew Hacker, *Two Nations Black and White, Separate, Hostile, Unequal* (New York: Ballantine Books, 1992), pp. 129–130.

4. Mel Elfin with Sarah Burke, "Race on Campus," *U.S. News & World Report*, April 19, 1993, p. 53.

5. Ibid., p. 52.

6. Ibid.

7. James Traub, "Can Separate Be Equal?," *Harper's Magazine*, June 1994, pp. 36–38.

8. Arthur M. Schlesinger, Jr., *The Disuniting of America* (New York: W. W. Norton & Co., 1992), p. 95.

9. Ibid.

10. Elfin with Burke, p. 54.

11. Schlesinger, p. 69.

12. "The Next to the Last Word on Political Correctness," *The New York Times*, December 11, 1993, p. 23.

## Chapter 6

1. *CNN World News Tonight*, May 10, 1994.

# Further Reading

Bullard, Sara. *Free At Last.* New York: Oxford University Press, 1993.

Cook, Fred J. *The Ku Klux Klan.* New York: Julian Messner, 1980.

Dudley, William and Charles Cozic, eds. *Racism in America.* San Diego, Calif.: Greenhaven Press, Inc., 1991.

Edwards, Gabrielle I. *Coping With Discrimination.* New York: Rosen Publishing Group, 1986.

Katz, William Loren. *The Invisible Empire.* Washington, D.C.: Open Hand Publishing, Inc., 1986.

Kosof, Anna. *The Civil Rights Movement and Its Legacy.* New York: Franklin Watts, 1989.

Leone, Bruno. *Racism: Opposing Viewpoints.* St. Paul, Minn.: Greenhaven Press, 1986.

McKissack, Patricia and Frederick. *Taking a Stand Against Racism and Racial Discrimination.* New York: Franklin Watts, 1990.

Pascoe, Elaine. *Racial Prejudice, Issues in American History.* New York: Franklin Watts, 1985.

# Index